Geoffrey Bradfield wishes to acknowledge his profound debt of gratitude to Paige Rense, editor-in-chief of *Architectural Digest,* for recognizing and publishing his work in the pages of her august magazine through the years. Without her professional generosity, this book would not have been possible.

- J.P.

Millennium Modern, *adj.;* mil-len'ni-um mod'ern; a term describing a style of interior design of the 1990's and the decade of the 2000's; derived from contemporary art and based generally on the reinterpretation of designs of the 1930's and 1940's and applied to furnishings, textiles, and interior and architectural design, etc., on the cusp of the third millennium.

- Geoffrey Bradfield

For Jesse –
with warmest wishes
William
April 04

Published and distributed internationally by
Bibliotheque: World Wide
11 Petria, Irvine, California 92606
Tel.: (949) 786-3913. Fax: (949) 786-8918
www.bibliothequeworldwide.com
www.bwwsociety.org

10 9 8 7 6 5 4 3 2 1

International Standard Book Number 1-882292-32-4

Typography and Graphic Design:
          Bibliotheque: World Wide, Irvine, California USA

Printed and bound in China

GEOFFREY BRADFIELD
DEFINING MILLENNIUM MODERN

by John Pellam

Principal Photographer: Durston Saylor

BIBLIOTHEQUE: WORLD WIDE

TABLE OF CONTENTS

INTRODUCTION

"To me, designing is really about providing magic. When someone views one of my interiors, I want the overall effect to be akin to the moment when archaeologist Howard Carter peered into King Tut's tomb and Lord Carnarvon asked, 'What do you see?' The reply was two words: 'Wondrous things.'"

- Geoffrey Bradfield

A Geoffrey Bradfield interior, like the man himself, never fails to impress or inspire the uninitiated. Those who know him are not in the least surprised by his creative dexterity. Bradfield's inimitable style, beautifully blending cultures, continents and centuries, undoubtedly springs from the contrasts inherent in the arc of his life. Raised on a farm in rural South Africa, and now residing at one of the most enviable addresses in Manhattan, Geoffrey Bradfield manages to strike a balance between humility and grandeur, continually bridging the distance between the past and present, but always designing -- and living -- for the moment.

Bradfield's singular style is predicated on the use of contemporary art, and his extraordinary interiors are often conceived as a foil to some of the most important and magnificent collections in existence today. Ever the ardent modernist, Bradfield is passionately committed to creating interiors that reflect our particular moment in time. However, it is not his intention to re-create period rooms -- Bradfield's unrivaled talent lies in coaxing traditional lines and arrangements into harmony with modern works of art, thereby yielding an energetic expression of the present. Within Geoffrey Bradfield's artfully designed rooms, utilitarian objects receive the same polished consideration as *objets d'art*. The stunning result is always an elegantly comfortable, coherent whole, one that marries form and function in a masterful synthesis Bradfield likes to refer to as "functional opulence."

Although his taste is impeccable and he has definitive ideas about the mood he seeks to create, Bradfield always designs with the client in mind. As antiques guru Bruce Newman, formerly the president of Newel Art Galleries in New York, puts it, "Geoffrey grasps the personality of the client, and he never decorates for himself. In my opinion, he is one of the exceptional designers working today -- one who fills the void left by the late Mark Hampton." Throughout his storied career, Bradfield's discerning eye has given him the opportunity to transform the interiors of many of the world's most eminent homes. As a young designer new to North America, he was singled out by Joan Mondale, wife of then-Vice President Walter Mondale, to plan the new layouts for the Vice Presidential home, which was being completely updated in an innovative break from tradition. Mrs. Mondale's serendipitous choice of Bradfield was a boon to the fledgling designer, thrusting the eager newcomer onto the American design stage. In the intervening years, Bradfield's special style has made its mark on illustrious homes throughout the United States, Canada, Mexico, Europe and the Orient. Among this roster was the major design overhaul of Gertrude Vanderbilt Whitney's exalted estate on Long Island, and his current collaboration on the complete restoration of the late King Hussein's regal mansion in Maryland. Recently, he received the prestigious commission of restoring the artistically significant long gallery in Edith Wharton's former country estate, The Mount, sensitively revitalizing one of America's most cherished landmarks.

Bradfield is esteemed for his unique ability to make even the most architecturally staid interior resonate with contemporary vigor, and as a result he is most often called upon to work on major landmark or award-winning contemporary buildings. Bradfield can maintain the magnificent beauty of a historical building while updating it with his astutely modernist sensibilities, just as he can warm the too-cold angles of a contemporary interior with the skillful introduction of a traditionally appointed arrangement. The princely scale of these residences gives Bradfield full reign to experiment with a broad spectrum of art and antiques. But more often than not, Bradfield's selections are confined to a handful of trusted dealers in New York, London and Paris, who expertly procure pieces to meet his exacting standards. One of the hallmarks of Geoffrey Bradfield's style is his ability to merge pieces of disparate periods and provenance into one spectacularly compelling arrangement. His mission, accomplished in each and every room he touches, is to treat the eye to an array of art and objects in juxtapositions never before imagined.

Upon the pages that follow, many wondrous things, indeed, abound. The volume you now hold in your hands is, in essence, a retrospective of the refined wizardry of Geoffrey Bradfield's work. Bradfield has said that the 21st century parallels his own quest for simplicity -- and his exquisitely restrained sense of design, evident upon each of the pages to follow, bears witness to that sentiment in a most eloquent manner. Bradfield is a modernist, constantly looking forward, yet never losing sight of the past.

The man who coined the term "Millennium Modern" is undoubtedly the most qualified to carry out its expression, which he does so authoritatively in each of his creations. As this era of Millennium Modern continues, Bradfield too will continue to innovate, to create, and, above all, to define the era in which we live.

- John Pellam

THE DESIGNER

Geoffrey Bradfield grew up on a farm in South Africa on the Indian Ocean, leaving home in his late teens to travel the world. After fulfilling his regimental army service, he toured India, Australia, Asia, Europe and America before returning to Johannesburg, all with an eye towards the ideal of ultimately living in New York City. In Johannesburg, the preternaturally talented Bradfield stood out among a vanguard of innovative young designers, and was the first amidst the burgeoning scene to receive international recognition. After seven years as an associate at two leading design firms, and ever in search of new challenges, Bradfield uprooted himself at the age of twenty-nine and made his way to Manhattan.

The ascendancy of Bradfield's career following his arrival in Manhattan was nothing short of meteoric. He got his start at the venerable McMillen, Inc., a firm whose prestigious projects during his tenure included the Kennedy Library in Boston and the residence of a young Queen Noor of Jordan. Bradfield subsequently joined Jay Spectre, Inc., with whom he forged a lasting partnership that endured until the latter's death in 1992. It was with Jay Spectre that Bradfield's singular aesthetic firmly took root and flourished. In addition to designing innumerable cover page interiors, he and Spectre became phenomenally successful as pioneers in product licensing, fabricating prototypes -- literally spanning the full gamut of home furnishings. And in the heady days of his early collaboration with Jay Spectre, his circle of friends and clients grew to encompass many of the bold-faced names of New York society. The ambitious boy from South Africa who was once transfixed in a dark theater by *Breakfast at Tiffany's* half a world away was now in a Fifth Avenue apartment entertaining Truman Capote.

Geoffrey Bradfield's social calendar now includes dining with Prince Charles at Windsor Castle and rubbing shoulders with the President of France and European elite at balls in Versailles. Bradfield has thrice been named one of the top 100 interior designers in the world by *Architectural Digest*. In addition, he has received numerous awards and accolades, has lectured at the Smithsonian, and makes frequent guest appearances on style-related television programs, all while working his magic on the homes, jets and yachts of his Fortune 500 clients, whom he deems "silent celebrities." Of course, his clients have a full voice when it comes to celebrating Bradfield's work, and as his reputation has grown, his workload has increased exponentially. But the unflappable designer takes it all in stride.

With a practiced hand, he fits new commissions into his brimming schedule with the same expertise he draws on to appoint a room. For Geoffrey Bradfield, challenge is its own reward.

Geoffrey Bradfield seated in the living
room of a recently completed installation
in Monterrey, Mexico.

A Suite at the Mayfair

Located on New York's Upper East Side, architect Costas Kondylis' 1925 Gothic masterpiece, the Mayfair Hotel, has been converted into seventy elegant private residences, one of which, featured here, is a design 'in praise of restraint.' Capturing Geoffrey Bradfield's own inimitable style, the apartment is the purest expression of his design principles.

Bradfield designed and introduced three pairs of eleven-foot pilasters to bring together the Classic architecture of the living room, and a silk and wool area rug, woven in China, as a creative reference to the Art Moderne period. The result is nothing less than an entertaining and surprising composite of humor, levity, and supreme sophistication, conjured with a seemingly artless simplicity.

An Archipenko bronze greets visitors in the entrance hall. Custom area rugs all but cover the dark hardwood floors. The walls are upholstered in celadon raw silk.

In the dining area, Geoffrey Bradfield's effective use of an extendable glass cantilevered dining table is shown in both aspects in the photographs above and at right. On top of the table in the image above, Diego Giacometti's playful cats hold lighted candles. A selection of wine flasks, created by South African glass blower Shirley Cloete, add an element of iridescence. At right is a bronze sculpture by Lynn Chadwick and, captured in the floor to ceiling mirrors, Mancini's blue 'Venus de Milo.'

In the bedroom (shown at right and on the previous two pages), Bradfield's palette of greens -- celadon, menthol and chartreuse -- create, in the designer's words, "calm, light, and a sense of uncluttered serene space." Throughout the residence, the most remarkable names in 20th century art can be found: Cocteau, Lalanne, Giacometti, Poillerat, Ruhlmann, Jean Arp, Milton Avery, Archipenko and Yves Klein. Yet there are built-in touches of madness, too: the powder room in jade green ultrasuede, framed in heavy metal studs and showcasing Cocteau's 'Hand of Poppies,' is pure theater.

A COLLECTOR'S AERIE

In the entrance at right, the elevator landing, Bradfield introduces a handkerchief ceiling stenciled in gold leaf squares, oak boiserie walls with a diamond veneer dado inlaid with bronze, and stone floors. Construction on the building was completed in 1929, inspiring Bradfield to include Art Deco in his design. By mirroring the south wall, he has created a feeling of infinity. A bronze and brushed steel console designed by Bradfield holds a 200 B.C. antiquity of the young King David; the pair of bronze wall sconces are 1930's, French.

Magnificent in both scale and location, this apartment occupies an entire floor in the tower of the Sherry-Netherland Hotel and offers extraordinary views of the city from virtually every room. Works by Degas, Renoir, and Matisse grace the walls of this home, but the serious collectors who live here have made 20th century masters the focal point of their exceptional *oeuvre,* and include Avery, Leger, Bourgeois, Dubuffet, Survage, Diebenkorn, Calder, Metzinger, Moore and Archipenko among their treasures. Geoffrey Bradfield skillfully played down his design in this apartment, yielding a quiet sophistication that complements the remarkable collection. In so doing, Bradfield has allowed the exuberance of the art its full voice.

Four centuries are spanned in the image at right, with a Louis XVI mantle, the 18th century gilt Irish mirror and the contemporary bronze by Étienne Beöthy, entitled 'A Drop of Rain and a Wave.' The willingness to experiment with unusual juxtapositions is evident throughout the interior.

This apartment was once the home of the legendary Claire Boothe Luce during the period when she was the American Ambassador to Italy. Geoffrey Bradfield's clients, however, did not require the vast proportions of the voluminous ballroom. In accordance with their needs, the designer converted this sixty-foot space into two rooms, utilizing approximately two-thirds of the space for the living room (shown on the preceding two pages) and devoting the remaining one-third to the library (shown on the following pages).

On the preceding pages, Bradfield had the living room walls upholstered in an ivory-colored watermark linen. Essentially a room in creams and whites, the predominant color introduction is the flame red and gold William Morris rug. The shape of a diamond is a recurring theme throughout the reception areas; although very subtle, it can be found in the upholstery, the quilted silk draperies and the boiserie.

On the following two pages, the tone of the gentleman's dressing room is set by the 19th century Japanese screen, which Geoffrey Bradfield acquired in Osaka from the Oriental connoisseur David Kidd.

Bradfield has a fondness for texture contrasts, rich exotic woods, burnished metals and lush textiles. He exploits these contrasts as a foil, highlighting the elements of fine design from many centuries. The library, above, is warm and intimate, paneled in oak veneer. A pair of custom designed bronze wall sconces display Ming roof tiles. A scarab vase by Lalique, Ruhlmann supper table, a set of Russian chairs and a 19th century geometric English needlepoint rug complete the picture.

For the master bedroom, Bradfield
upholstered the walls in a shell pink raw
silk in a checkered pattern. The bed
throw and draperies are in harlequin
pastel-colored silk taffeta. Of particular
interest in the room is a signed, gilded
writing table by Rateau, a pair of 1930's
crystal sconces by Baccarat (formerly in
the collection of Cole Porter) and a fine
oil painting by Marie Laurencin.

At left, the vanity table in the lady's dressing room enjoys an exceptional view, looking down upon the romantic mansard roof of the Plaza Hotel. Bradfield continued the shell pink raw silk wall upholstery into this adjoining room, repeating the accenting draperies.

A LANDMARK LIMESTONE IN NEW YORK

"I would like to think this interior captures our moment in time," says Geoffrey Bradfield of this distinctive design. The following pages reveal an abstract painting by one of South Africa's foremost artists, Karel Nel, titled 'Ancestral Void,' Louise Nevelson's white wall sculpture, Jeff Koons' 'Puppy,' and Lalanne's 'l'Oiseau Bleu.' Bradfield describes this interior as "transcending several centuries." It features Louis XVI boiserie, Art Moderne furnishings, and an oval Aubusson rug designed by Bradfield -- all juxtaposed with contrasting custom-designed Lucite, glass and brushed steel furniture.

This distinguished limestone townhouse, just steps from Fifth Avenue, was originally built for the Drexel family in 1903. Designed by Horace Trumbauer, the six-story residence was later divided into eight apartments. The living room of this duplex was formerly the mansion's library. Geoffrey Bradfield's signature use of art is immediately apparent with the Kenneth Noland striped vertical painting. The sixteen-foot ceilings are, in the designer's words, the apartment's "glamour statement," while the overall interior design creates "a spiritual cohesion between disparate centuries." The aesthetic summation of this apartment is, ultimately, Contemporary.

INDIAN KNOLL, GREENWICH

This Greenwich residence is signature Geoffrey Bradfield. In an estate section known for its traditional mansions, an alien presence of ultra-sophistication sits like a spaceship settled in a meadow. This 21st century home, which exemplifies Bradfield's attitude toward futuristic high-tech, encapsulates the designer's quest for simplicity. Contrasts in colors and cultures and hard and soft surfaces are set against a virtual canvas of the New England forest afforded by the soaring, twenty-foot high windows. In every facet of this dazzling home, color, light and form coalesce, revealing Bradfield's extraordinary vision of what it means to design for the 21st century.

The elegant living room is framed by a sleek, two-story glass wall that looks out over the pool and landscaped grounds. Contrasting with the stark concrete walls is an eclectic grouping of leather sofas and plush Art Deco club chairs, including a pair from the ocean liner *Normandie*, upholstered in jewel-toned mohair velvets. A Deco-inspired custom carpet of large black peonies on a beige field injects drama. Adding to the mix are an important collection of tribal art and a number of large floral canvases by Lowell Nesbitt.

740 PARK AVENUE

In the regal entrance at left, Geoffrey Bradfield upholstered the walls in rich scarlet mohair velvet as a backdrop for the striking Archipenko sculpture, 'The Gondolier,' which graces the gently curving stairway. The designer conceived the bronze and crystal sphere stair rail and executed the stair carpeting with the same daring use of scarlet, accented with a black chevroned border.

Once home to the Rockefellers and considered to be one of the top seven residential buildings in New York, this 1929 landmark was designed by the great architect Rosario Candela. Geoffrey Bradfield's artful interior complements the magnificent proportions of the building, yet, in keeping with the times, bears the imprint of the designer's modernist sensibilities. In the living room (above), arched window surrounds and matching display niches enhance the contours of the space. The designer continued the arch theme with the ingenious acquisition of the Christo painting of le Pont Neuf, which hangs above the piano.

The library, shown on the following pages, illustrates Bradfield's masterful skill with color and fabric. The designer upholstered the walls in chocolate-brown mohair velvet, and then used a honey-colored oak for the shutters and pediment-topped bookcases as a relief in color and texture. The contrasting honey color is repeated in the area rug and the channeled leather sofa, which in turn is accented by the designer's use of kilim rugs from which the occasional pillows were crafted. The 19th century primitive mask hung between the bookcases accentuates the tribal feeling of the kilim fabric.

At left is a view of the dining room from the main entry hall. In this richly appointed room, Bradfield began his design with the stenciled wood floor, upon which he placed a round antique Savonnerie rug. The English table is a period piece, as are the chairs, which are upholstered in woven horsehair. Against the far wall is one of a pair of floor-length 'cracked ice' mirrors, which the designer had crafted from highly polished steel. For the master bedroom, displayed in the photograph above, Bradfield selected a portfolio of framed lithographs by Léonor Fini, and designed the Oriental-style charcoal and brushed steel writing desk. The walls are upholstered in a soft cantaloupe-colored silk.

A Dining Room
in Yellow

Geoffrey Bradfield has used a warm palette of soft yellows for this secluded room. As accent pieces, he introduced a whimsical Roy Lichtenstein sculpture as a centerpiece on the tabletop, and an important white Louise Nevelson construction over the mantlepiece. Through his former partner, the late Jay Spectre, the designer came to know Louise Nevelson fairly well, and wryly recalls her as "a charmingly eccentric character, who once arrived for an installation attired in a full-length sable; like a tool box, the deep coat pockets were amply stocked with hammer and nails for that morning's work."

This room typifies a distinctive style Geoffrey Bradfield embraces. Here he has used a rich, dark table with light, chalk colored painted chairs, thereby avoiding an overly 'matched' look and creating a contrast both in texture and color. Overhead, the 1930's French rock crystal and gilt vermeil chandelier is balanced by the subtle light filtering in through the gauzed window and the soft illumination of the wall sconces.

This room illustrates Geoffrey Bradfield's commitment to creating interiors that reflect what he describes as a "cross-pollination of the arts over many centuries."

AN OLD WESTBURY ESTATE

Originally the home of Gertrude Vanderbilt Whitney, this fine example of Georgian-style architecture was built in 1925 by the firm of Stewart, Walker and Gillette. Ms. Whitney is an integral part of American lore, and it was her passion for modern art that led her to found the legendary Whitney Museum and become a leading champion of 20th century American art. When the main house was renovated and two new wings added, Geoffrey Bradfield was called upon to embellish the artistically-significant residence with his modernist sensibilities.

Bradfield maintained the elegant stair rail (a "gem," according to the designer), but removed the original wood floors, replacing them with beige limestone and black granite. Custom-designed coffered inserts embellish the previously plain ceiling. A bronze Anthony Caro sculpture graces the entrance hall, while Fernand Leger's 1953 painting "L'Atelier de Chevareuse" hangs above the mantle in the living room. In keeping with the spirit of the estate's original owner, the residence houses an ever-expanding collection of art, including paintings by Frank Stella and Francisca Sutil, and sculptures by Henry Moore, Barbara Hepworth and Jean Arp.

Of his design for the bedroom, Bradfield says he no longer sees a reason to hide television screens, as the newest models are "streamlined and beautiful" and should be used as they are. The Louis XVI style of the area encompassing the pool, gym and spa was inspired by the architecture of Royaumont Abbey. The renovated attic, formerly the servants' quarters, was furnished in the Adirondack style, transforming it into a fun and spacious game room for the clients' children.

THE MOUNT IN THE BERKSHIRES

Placed on fluted pedestals, a classic collection of bronzes by contemporary sculptor Sabin Howard anchors the room in four corners. A pair of over-scaled iron lanterns, repeating the leaf motif, hang from the barrel-vaulted ceiling.

American literary giant Edith Wharton built The Mount in 1902 according to the architecture and design decrees set forth in her book *The Decoration of Houses* (co-written with Ogden Codman, Jr. in 1897, the seminal book is still in print). When Wharton's one-time country estate was elevated to landmark status, Geoffrey Bradfield received the prestigious commission of restoring the long gallery. In designing this chamber, Bradfield's intent was to retain the original character of the house while introducing a new look that would meet his contemporary tastes. Seeking to bring the space to life, Bradfield settled on a decidedly Art Moderne feel with a spare, crisp interior. Using a palette of ivories and celadon greens, he highlighted the ornamentation of the barrel-vaulted ceiling. In addition, he designed four exotic baroque settees upholstered in heavy Venetian embroideries, which sit in front of custom relief plaster panels of entwined leaves.

Bradfield's final design fulfills his ongoing pursuit of interiors that embody integrity, wit and beauty. The deceptively simple result was borne of a partnership between the timeless architecture of The Mount and Bradfield's innovative approach to contemporary design.

800 FIFTH AVENUE

Built on the site of the Dodge Mansion, the last of the great homes to fall to the wrecking ball in the mid-70's, this Fifth Avenue apartment exemplifies Geoffrey Bradfield's bold use of art and showcases the designer's infatuation with streamlined forms. One's attention is immediately captured by the large Ernest Fiene oil painting, which dominates the main wall of the living room. (The self-portrait depicts the artist at work in his studio overlooking the construction site of the Empire State Building.) Bradfield continued his design with sculptural displays of Art Deco forms in both subtle and exaggerated groupings, to intrigue the eye. The 1930's Deco feeling is augmented by original designs by Bradfield and his provocative use of edgy ultramodern lighting -- illumination, according to the designer, being *the* aesthetic element most effective in evoking glamour.

Shown above: the classic Deco cabinet belonged to HRH The Duke of Windsor, and previously complemented his bedroom suite at the Waldorf Towers; to the right of the cabinet hangs a 1930's painting by American artist Fanny Hill Smith. The card table at left is from the grillroom of the ocean liner *Queen Mary*.

500 PARK AVENUE

The presence of this award-winning structure, built in 1986 by Skidmore, Owings and Merrill, caused a stir when it appeared on venerable Park Avenue. This apartment has a monastic feel in keeping with the stark contemporary architecture of the building. To achieve the minimalist interior which Geoffrey Bradfield sought, he eliminated the mundane and exiled the ordinary. Adept at manipulating space, Bradfield conceived the living room as a form of art gallery, where collections could be displayed. The understatedly lavish walls, made of a blend of creme and white cement, perfectly offset the use of textures in the room: the glossy lacquers, the smooth glass, and the rich woods of the primitive art collections. The floors are faded parquet, and covered with large sisal area rugs. Bradfield kept fitted cabinetry to a minimum except for a pair of custom-designed, highly lacquered white vitrines, which were mounted above existing exposed A/C units. The display adds dramatic architecture to the west wall of the living room, and showcases to great effect the collection of African tribal headrests.

At left: As one enters the hall or long gallery, one is confronted by a 12-foot canvas by Kenneth Noland (left wall) and a sensual bronze cheetah by Gwynn Murrill. Noland's masterly discipline and serenity of clean lines stands in stark contrast to Murrill's fluid feline.

An ardent perfectionist, Bradfield is never satisfied. In his unending search for the new, he discovered the work of Hugo Bastidas, an emergent painter born in Ecuador, and used a selection of this artist's black-and-white oils to dramatic effect in this interior. Simple bound grass rugs and Art Deco French bergeres slipcovered in crisp mattress ticking bring to mind the charm and simplicity of the provinces. The master bedroom (at right) boasts a Venetian Art Moderne screen of costumed blackamoors and a Gary Kahn cubistic white column sculpture.

A Manhattan Pied-a-Terre

"I was inspired by the modern lines of the post-war architecture," says Geoffrey Bradfield of the compact pied-a-terre. The splendid view, overlooking Park Avenue's Ritz Tower, reminded Bradfield of the set of the old black-and-white film *Deception*, starring Bette Davis. With this in mind, the designer employed similar design references, like horizontal levelor shades and sleek banquettes with exposed parquet floors. He then adroitly integrated a variety of works of art into the design, including Arnoldo Pomodoro's 'Bronze Sphere,' an Andy Warhol silkscreen and sculptor Menashe Kadishman's shepherdless 'Herd of Sheep' on top of the round dining table. Note Bradfield's innovative device of a hinged bookcase door, which cleverly conceals a powder room.

The entry hall features a striking bronze floor sculpture by Carroll Todd, contrasted by a playful red tabletop figure by Russian artist Grisha Bruskin, and a Robert Motherwell watercolor on the left wall.

THE BERESFORD

A stylish apartment in the majestic Beresford, the 'Grand Dowager' among a roster of great buildings surrounding Central Park, this sixteenth floor aerie is dominated by the client's exceptional art collection. Upon entering the dramatic space, one's attention is immediately drawn to Louise Nevelson's 'Rain Forest Column XXX' at the far end of the gallery, while (at left), Arnoldo Pomodoro's shimmering 1996 work, 'Gyroscopia' anchors the west end. Atop the Neoclassical painted and parcel-gilt console table is a rare collection of 5th century B.C. Greek vessels.

Geoffrey Bradfield was intent upon exploiting the dramatic potential of the imposing entrance hall, which can be accessed by seven different doors. With an eye towards imprinting a classical signature on the residence, the apartment was completely remodeled, from the marble and wood floors to its mouldings and various architectural details. Throughout the apartment, modern works of art sit comfortably alongside traditional pieces culled from several continents and spanning centuries, producing an interior that is decidedly contemporary.

Geoffrey Bradfield found the long Neoclassical console table in Europe, and had the piece illuminated from below so that it appears to float upon a subtle cushion of light.

Fernando Botero's 1989 work, 'Homage a Canova,' is shown above. The previous pages display French artist Jean Dubuffet's enigmatic 'Figure V,' a 1974 study in black and white. The dining room, shown right, is elegantly accented with a French 1940's Art Moderne gunmetal and gilt chandelier. For the Chinese Chippendale chairs, Bradfield selected a sienna woven horsehair offset with a detailed bronze nailhead upholstery technique.

Hanging above the mantle is Kenneth Noland's 1997-98 circle painting 'Six,' the first painting Bradfield acquired with the client. The work formed the nucleus of the entire collection featured within this remarkable apartment.

A TOWNHOUSE IN THE CAPITAL

In the library, a fully upholstered island seating, designed by Bradfield, backs up into an exotic Regency sofa table. Bradfield chose a warm bird's eye maple to panel the walls, and adds a final, fanciful note to the room by appropriating the design of playing cards in the upholstery and carpet.

Beyond the stately embassies and national monuments of Washington DC lies the cosmopolitan residential enclave of Georgetown. The imposing scale of this townhouse reflects the spirit of its venerable location. The interior has an attitude of eclecticism. The entrance hall, with its marble floors and geometric ceiling, sets the stage for what is to follow: the double-height volume immediately impresses its grandeur upon the visitor, while the custom-designed stair ballustrade, inspired by the Art Nouveau period, introduces the visual aesthetic.

The intricate metalwork of the brushed steel and bronze rail, the centerpiece of the home, is set off against refined pale linen walls, illustrating Geoffrey Bradfield's understated sense of design. Art Nouveau references continue throughout the home as a recurrent, unifying theme. In every room, Bradfield's strong affinity for blending contemporary aspects with early 20th century design is expertly borne out.

The first floor reception rooms demonstrate Bradfield's contemporary interpretation of traditionalism. The media room is paneled in an exotic veneer of Macassar ebony with two seating areas; one faces the media wall and the other the swimming pool and grounds. Vitrines hold a collection of pre-Columbian art.

Bradfield uses unusual juxtapositions of textures, colors and carefully chosen antiques to convey a modern sensibility in a traditionally appointed home. A monochromatic dining room houses the amusing combination of a Picasso crayon drawing next to a contemporary painting from Santa Fe. Hanging overhead, a French bronze and opaque glass chandelier echoes the Art Nouveau spirit.

The master bedroom is, in essence, a room in cremes and whites. Of particular interest: The French Art Nouveau bedroom suite, the 1930's copper and crystal sconces over the mantlepiece and a charming pencil drawing by Fernando Botero.

A CONNOISSEUR'S LAIR

At left, Archipenko's bronze and Edvard Munch's painting reside in harmony with the museum quality Queen Anne furniture of this finely appointed dining room.

Once again, in a manner in which he is so skilled, Geoffrey Bradfield has eloquently brought together elements from divergent centuries to create a perfectly contemporary setting, accented by Art Deco chairs, rich exotic woods and lush fabrics. Walls upholstered in a luxurious mohair serve as a canvas for the display of a varied collection of paintings, drawings, bronzes and *objets d'art*.

Against this rich backdrop, a melding of Edvard Munch paintings and drawings and exquisite bronzes by Archipenko and Maillol can be found. Bradfield designed the floor covering in a black-and-beige checkerboard, crafted in a carved cut pile on loop technique, to create a buoyant visual field in the room. The end result, somewhat understated in the designer's words, is "the library of a gentleman."

A PENTHOUSE IN THE ROCKIES

At left, a brilliantly colored Sam Francis acrylic situated over the bed is flanked by a pair of Diego Giacometti bronze figurative lamps. On the following pages: Bradfield customized the entire dining room, designing everything from the architectural elements to the long flowing draperies. The designer used a technique called book-matching for two round dining tables and matching chairs. He chose beautiful flitches of veneer and had them laid out in a dazzling sunburst pattern. The tables are inlaid with brushed steel and are set upon brushed steel pedestals.

"Sprawling and modernist" is how Geoffrey Bradfield describes this penthouse in the heart of Calgary. Confronted with 7500 square feet of raw space, Bradfield created a seductive interior that evokes the distinguished atmosphere of an exclusive men's club. The elegant entrance gives way to a subdued open-plan apartment that exploits the breathtaking views of the city and the Canadian Rockies in the distance. The myriad architectural references to the 1930's, the stepped ceiling, the David Hockney collage, the Jim Dine bronze and the marble and metal inlay floor create a dramatic stage that is impressive but not intimidating, cordial yet sumptuous.

A High Rise in Bluegrass Country

Bradfield accented this section of the penthouse with pillars crafted in zebrawood. Banded with polished steel, this exotic wood is reprised in the fireplace to house an illuminated surround. A modernist painting by Ilya Bolotowsky hangs above the fireplace. The chairs match those seen by the designer during a visit to the Paris apartment of Paloma Picasso.

Overlooking acres of beautiful Cherokee Park, this Louisville penthouse is all about surprise. Entering the space is like stepping onto a customized yacht, exquisitely appointed with exotic lacquered woods, rich fabrics and sleek metal finishes. An assemblage of rare objects and collectibles fill Geoffrey Bradfield's streamlined interior, yet nothing detracts from the sense of serenity. A 19th century Rimpa School Japanese screen is shown above. Don Carlos Miguel Berrocal's 'Romeo and Juliet' sits on one of a pair of consoles Bradfield designed in green marble and polished steel.

Bradfield positioned a pre-Colombian primitive figure on the coffee table, a perfect balance to the pair of lamps which he fashioned from pre-Colombian clay vessels. The fabulous 1935 gold lacquer relief screen, 'The Taming of the Horse,' by French artist Jean Dunand, originally graced the smoking room of the luxury liner the *Normandie*.

A Cottage in Tuxedo Park

In the dining room, Bradfield designed the lacquer credenza and steel and glass dining tables. The room is enhanced by a 1930's portrait by Ellen Emmitt Rand of Emily Davie. The sitter was a close personal friend of the designer.

Nestled amid the Ramapo Mountains of New York State lies the exclusive gated community of Tuxedo Park. Established in 1886 by Pierre Lorillard, the tobacco millionaire and sportsman, this elegant enclave is situated on approximately 5,000 idyllic acres surrounding three sparkling lakes. Architect Bruce Price designed the community around a common clubhouse, and the site became the destination spot for the 'New York Four Hundred.' Price's daughter Emily Post was born and lived her life within the rarefied world of the park, and it was here she wrote her famous book of etiquette, which remains a classic to this day. It was also here that Lorillard's son Griswold first donned a black-and-white party suit that would come to be known as the tuxedo.

The quality of life has changed little since Lorillard established the Park, and Geoffrey Bradfield decided to build his country retreat in this setting. He chose as his site three acres overlooking Tuxedo Lake, the largest of the three bodies of water, and used Andrea Palladio's Villa Pisani outside Vicenza as an inspiration. "The idea of building a house on classical principles crystallized a long time ago," Bradfield says. "I have an affinity for the cleanness of classical spaces; there is something very uncontrived about them." The architecture of the home is suffused with a sense of playfulness and fun, as if it were the smaller house built off to the side of a more grandiose mansion. "This house is more like a folly on a large estate," Bradfield says. "It's not as serious as the big house would be. It has pretensions, but the pretensions are mischievous."

The entire house follows the fall of the land: entrance hall down to gallery and gallery onto terrace. In a pair of octagonal rooms, designed in keeping with the Palladian principles, oversized windows and doors seamlessly integrate the outdoors with the interior, generously allowing for sweeping views of the hillside and the peaceful lake. A silkscreen by Man Ray is set into the mirror over the mantle, while two life-sized, fiberglass sculptures by Muriel Castanis are a spectral presence in the entrance hall.

Bradfield stenciled the walls of the dark green library in Russian motifs chosen from 18th century icons. "I wanted one to feel as if one was inside a Fabergé egg," says the designer. On the coffee table is a 1930's silver sculpture by Karl Hagenauer.

"My late partner, Jay Spectre, said to me that building one's own home was one of the great privileges of life, and indeed, building this first home was a growing experience," says Bradfield. "It was an opportunity to be perfectly selfish and create exactly what I wanted. I could put into practice my sympathy for architectural balance and symmetry and introduce influences from the 1920's and 1930's as a backdrop to new-age art. What I wanted to do was capture the best of our time. We are, with certainty, living in a fascinating chapter of design."

Above: Known as the 'Tuxedo Room,' one of the four upstairs bedrooms is decorated in black and white and dominated by a giant spherical window that looks out onto the lake and distant mountains.

A House in Notting Hill

At right, a Jim Dine lithograph hangs above the mantel in the living room. In the blue room, a dipthyque by South African artist Brian Bradshaw follows the contour of the sectional seating.

Notting Hill in London has become a mecca for young aristocrats, models and movie stars like Elle McPherson, Claudia Schiffer and her husband, film producer Matthew Vaughn. This elegant residence faces onto Pembridge Square. Built in the mid-19th century, it boasts fifteen-foot ceilings and lavish ornamental mouldings. Geoffrey Bradfield strove to retain the old world charm while infusing the space with his contemporary vision. The result is one of ultra-sophistication. He designed the mantlepiece of brushed steel, which stands five-and-a-half feet tall, to receive a pair of limestone relief nudes which date from the 18th century. The collection of contemporary art is a cross-pollination of American post-war and renowned South African artists.

A FURTHER LANE ESTATE, EAST HAMPTON

One of the most sought-after addresses in East Hampton, this park-like sixteen-acre estate sits above the sand dunes fronting the Atlantic Ocean. A half-mile-long gravel drive, lined with shady pin oaks, guides one toward the main house, which overlooks the estate's driving range, tennis courts, indoor and outdoor pools, and lush vegetation.

Above: A captivating bronze sculpture by Chinese artist Ju Ming can be seen through the breakfast room window, settled amid a glass-enclosed atrium.

"What makes the house not ordinary is the scale," says Bradfield. "It's amplified. The central hall is one hundred and sixty feet long and ten feet wide. Against a textured foil of seafoam green, Bradfield married a lively 19th century Mongolian kilim with Frank Stella's brilliantly colored oil on canvas and Roy Lichtenstein's 'Lily Pond.' The Chinese furnishings are museum-quality Huang Hua Li.

On the following pages: The cavernous living room, monumental in scale but welcoming, boasts an uncommonly high ceiling. Bright colors offset minimalist furnishings to create the most striking effects. On the right wall, Bradfield has placed Helen Frankenthaler's huge eight-by-twenty-four foot 1973 oil on canvas, 'Copper Afternoon,' the colors of which are superbly contrasted with the designer's use of pungent cantaloupe and chartreuse upholstery.

The photograph at left reveals the spectacular ocean view as framed by the soaring geometric ceiling and sculpture-like stacked stone fireplace. In the image above, Bradfield has selected sculptor Jean Arp's cubist bronze, 'The Rose Eater,' for the tabletop and a strong, horizontal eighteen foot Kenneth Noland oil on canvas to hang above the sofa.

On the following pages, one of a pair of exceptional 18th century Japanese screens flanks the dining room, depicting the Emperor's Royal Stables. Bradfield upholstered the walls in melon watermark linen; as accent pieces, in front of the screen is a rich red Raul Valdivieso sculpture, 'Seed,' while a set of brass Georgian candlesticks adds an elegant balance to the scene.

A PALM BEACH LAKEFRONT MANSION

"The excitement of design," says Bradfield, "is that it is not an exact science. It is not life threatening if an error occurs. There are so many ways to design a room." At left, the forecourt leading to the rotunda entry hall.

This exceptional home was designed by Maurice Fatio in 1927. Geoffrey Bradfield's extensive renovation expanded the existing structure to 22,000 square feet -- triple the original size. Above the front door in the limestone arch is a Renaissance ceramic sculpture of angels by della Robbia. The entrance hall is triple-volume, accessing three floors. Beneath the sweep of the gracious staircase, Bradfield placed an Anthony Caro sculpture, 'Procession,' upon a baroque gilt table, while a magnificent Louis XVI gilded lantern hangs overhead. Taking his inspiration from Madrid's Palacio de Lira, Bradfield designed the ornate plaster mouldings and coffered ceilings, which are a consistent architectural theme throughout.

At left, the reception hall has been extended to triple
its previous size. Bradfield retained the original Gothic
arches, which were salvaged from the Phipps Estate.
He commissioned a stonemason to recast two
additional pairs of window frames to match. Of note is
the minstrel gallery which is used by the clients -- who
pilot their own private jet -- as a chart room to map
out flight schedules. In an amusing move, Bradfield
used a hot coral fresco on the walls and a large paisley
Arabesque rug. One has the sense of floating above the
gallery as if on a magic carpet.

On the following pages, the great room, measuring sixty feet by forty feet, is part of the sprawling
new addition. Because of its mammoth scale, Bradfield was anxious that it not take on the appear-
ance of an airplane hanger. He designed a tray ceiling of plaster coffers to maintain a residential feel
and anchored the room with two seating areas defined by a pair of Directoire-style area rugs. When
it came to the dining room, Bradfield blended his own taste for simplicity with 'the grand tradition.'
The designer used seven pairs of classical columns, an ornate coffered ceiling and Versailles hardwood floors. In contrast to this formality, he introduced sculptures by contemporary artists Lynn
Chadwick and Fernando Botero. "The room has oxygen," says Bradfield, "it has a light, almost
transparent feeling. The textures are luxe but the patterns are geometric."

A DUPLEX AT 400 SOUTH OCEAN

Left, a place for art: A pair of bronze lifeguards by Aurora Canero gaze at the magnificent ocean view. Above: Beneath a brilliantly colored diamond oil on canvas by Kenneth Noland is a bronze sculpture by Lynn Chadwick.

Designed by the eminent architect Edward Durell Stone, this duplex is located on Palm Beach's 'Mansion Row,' a three-mile stretch of Atlantic beachfront. Geoffrey Bradfield has created a strikingly original interior, artfully fitting disparate pieces together in a simply unified whole. "For me, modern design is the most intriguing, but I am not interested in the 'icy cold' variety," says Bradfield. "I attempt to achieve a more rooted, tactile brand of modernism, embracing comfort, form and function." The furniture here, uniformly low, is covered smartly in touchable white cotton mixes. The clean lines of the apartment create the perfect showcase for art. This is dramatically apparent on the following pages, illustrated by Bradfield's authoritative use of Andy Warhol's 'Double Elvis,' which powerfully dominates the north wall.

At left, an amusing gold sculpture by surrealist Salvador Dali, 'La Persistence de la Memoire,' complements French artist Jean Cocteau's crayon drawing. In this bedroom, Bradfield continued his use of light colors, from the sisal floor covering to the beige-and-white striped Art Moderne chair. Above, the living room and tranquil ocean view, reflected in the overscaled gold framed mirror.

AN OCEANFRONT ESTATE, PALM BEACH

Eighteen-foot vaulted arches grace the loggia, elegantly framing nature's unrivaled canvas. Bradfield contrasted his design for the loggia's sandstone table by introducing dark green rattan and rawhide dining chairs.

There are those rare places in the world where architecture and natural terrain are in complete harmony, Venice being one of them. *La Serenissimo*, from which this estate takes its name, is one such Eden. Four acres of lush vegetation and tropical palms surround the courtly 25,000 square foot mansion fronting onto turquoise Atlantic waters.

"I've undertaken far more extensive renovations in my career, but the significance of this project lay in the challenge of creating an interior for a singular collection of contemporary and modern art," says Geoffrey Bradfield. "By being spared the task of knocking down walls and redistributing vast spaces, I was free to apply my energies to more subtle details. I consider the results to be a high-water mark among my design accomplishments." Crafted from coral stone quarried from the offshore reefs, the staircase serves as a dramatic accent to the Roy Lichtenstein oil on canvas on the left wall, while Lee Krasner's collage commands one's attention from above. Beneath the rising staircase is a Robert Graham sculpture beside a reclining nude by artist Tom Wesselmann; a 4th century marble horsehead is set on top of an 18th century Irish table.

Left: 'Matador,' an important oil on canvas by Fernando Botero, hangs above the mantlepiece, while the mobile by artist Alexander Calder rests upon the Diego Giacometti coffee table. At John Hobbs' showroom in London, during an extensive shopping trip in Europe with his clients, Bradfield happened upon an exquisite set of four early 19th century gilt chairs. This extraordinary acquisition became the anchor of the vast living room. Says the designer, "These chairs were of the caliber required to rise to the stature of the art collection." At right, a Roy Lichtenstein bronze sits on a marble sofa table.

Of particular interest in this highly edited furniture collection is the fact that all the Diego Giacometti pieces were acquired by the designer from the studio of the artist. Bradfield's late partner, Jay Spectre, had forged a friendship, beginning in the late 1960's, with Diego. On almost every shopping trip to Paris over the years, Spectre would visit the artists's mildly chaotic studio at 54 rue du Moulin Vert. Bradfield was fortunate to be included in many of these memorable pilgrimages. They would usually arrive with a gift of Kentucky whiskey, which Diego favored, and invariably would have lunch together at the Café Barola, one of the artist's favorite haunts. Says Bradfield, "It was inspirational spending time with one of the world's great artists and in many ways, a turning point in my life."

One of four seating areas in the living room, an 18th century Russian gilt and crimson lacquer table holds an exquisite blue glass St. Petersburg clock, a Lalique salver and a bronze sculpture by Jean Arp. On the following pages, art prevails in sumptuous settings. In the library, Hans Hoffman's oil on canvas hangs above the mantle-piece, flanked by a pair of Diego Giacometti lamps. Of particular note is the Russian chair, inlaid with bronze, from Czar Nicolas' library at the Winter Palace, backed up to a French Charles X desk.

"My task was not to alter the house's form, but rather its tone," explains Bradfield. "My contribution was predicated on the use of art; I designed the rooms *around* the works of art and sculpture, not vice versa, which is as it should be." On pages 174 and 175: An oil on canvas by French artist Albert Gleizes graces a collection of 18th century garniture in the dining room, and holds equal weight to its opposite wall. Its complement is a 1921 seascape by Thomas Hart Benton that once belonged to the Pennsylvania Academy of Fine Arts. The painting hangs above a Gustavian console enhanced by a Tang camel and a Caldwell clock. On the pages following, Bradfield added color to the monochromatic master bedroom by featuring works by the artist Willem de Kooning on the far wall and a striking oil on canvas by Adolph Gottlieb to the right.

A House on North Lake Way

This informal beach house is Geoffrey Bradfield's winter home in Florida. The designer describes his residence as "a study in contrasts, a brashly geometrically themed design using circles and squares as referenced by the cubic art and round rug and tables." It was, he says, his goal to create "an amalgam of visual wit."

In the entry hall at left, one is immediately struck by the 18th century marble head of Athena, flanked by Mexican artist Pedro Freidberg's gilded chairs, while in the image reflected in the mirror, Fernando Botero's bronze cat is seated on top of the console table. On the following two pages is the living room which Bradfield has furnished with, among other select pieces, a pair of Mies van der Rohe daybeds and two matching coffee tables that once belonged to the late decorating legend, Elsie de Wolfe.

In the detail photograph above, a whimsical pair of sheep by French artist François-Xavier Lalanne.

Bradfield's work is synonymous with his style for incorporating splendid art into his interiors. "I was seeking a poetic collection of simple, elegant forms -- acquisitions that are both sensuous and operatic. The space is scattered with an array of what I like to call play things," says Bradfield. A dramatic example is the imposing marble sculpture by Sacha Sosno placed squarely in the denim blue library. The cabana yields striking visual effects and bold imagery: the focal point and inspiration is Charles Baskerville's 'Sultan on Horseback,' originally from the breakfast room of Mar-A-Lago, the Palm Beach estate of the late Marjorie Merriwether Post. The North African color palette drawn from the painting is nothing short of a 'tropical punch,' with hot mango yellows and shocking Schiaparelli pinks, set against a faux Moorish colonnade.

The story of this very personal collection would be incomplete without a further note: anyone who knows Geoffrey Bradfield also knows well of his passion for art and his fascination with those who create it. The designer had long wanted to meet Francois Xavier Lalanne, the French sculptor who created the sheep featured in his home, and most of all to join the artist and his wife in their famous garden outside of Paris, which is filled with a Noah-like collection of the couple's fanciful animal sculptures. By chance, while staying at the Crillon in Paris, Bradfield received a surprise phone call very early one morning from his friend, renowned art dealer Jean-Gabriel Mitterrand, with an invitation to breakfast with the artist and his wife. The venerable pair have become rather reclusive over the last decade, receiving very few people. Bradfield was, of course, delighted at this opportunity and immediately cancelled all his appointments, spending several magical hours at their extraordinary house.

BREAKERS ROW

At left, the dramatic entrance to the apartment with Aurora Canero's indolent bronze sculpture 'Canoe' floating against an arched backdrop of intense coral, The brushed steel and glass coffee table was designed by Bradfield.

The Breakers Hotel in Palm Beach is the undisputed 'Grande Dame' of this luxury resort. Breakers Row is the exclusive residential adjunct to the hotel, offering all of its finest services.

In this interior, with broad brushstrokes, Geoffrey Bradfield has humorously alluded to the history of modern art. What makes the residence so enormously appealing is the simplicity of its design, the emphasis on comfort and the joyous focus on nature and art. Playing into his established vernacular, Bradfield created a tranquil setting for his clients' edgy contemporary collection.

A PAVILION BY THE SEA

In the dining area above, a hand-beaten silver bowl by Gilbert Poillerat graces the Jacques Emile Ruhlmann credenza. Bradfield designed the two round dining tables with an Art Moderne reference in mind. He commissioned the twin centerpieces from Buccellati; they are composed of clustered nautical shells in vermeil.

One of only fifty oceanfront properties in Palm Beach, this 1970's Regency style limestone needed wall-to-wall work. What it already had in its favor was a series of breathtaking views from each of the main rooms of the house. Geoffrey Bradfield was inspired: "The sun-drenched light and serene, calming colors are so like the Indian Ocean where I grew up. I immediately envisioned a beautiful pavilion by the sea, in a resort I know very well."

The part of the house fronting the ocean, comprised of the living room, loggia, dining room and library, was completely restructured to take full advantage of the spectacular vista. A thicket of marble columns obstructed the panorama; Bradfield removed all twenty-two of them, as well as the doors. He reframed three of the entries with understated, elegant twin pillars, and installed beige Italian marble flooring to visually unify the area.

The open plan living space is filled with art treasures. An abstract painting by Dubuffet is highlighted above a Swedish banquette covered in striped fabric. The dramatic flow of the large oil by Joan Mitchell in the loggia contrasts with the crisp, straight lines of a Barbara Hepworth bronze.

Bradfield designed the pool deck, artfully placing Robert Graham's bronze sculpture of a female nude center stage. The master bedroom overlooks the pool area and features an overscaled chaise for two, covered in a large blue-and-white silk check with matching draperies and bed throw. Like the radiant sea outside its doors, each room of the house is fluid and graceful, expertly rendered by a skilled practitioner of modern style and design.

A RESIDENCE ON LAKE WORTH

Left: A large oil on canvas 'target' painting by Kenneth Noland commands the north wall. A lucky bid bought a set of eighteen Art Moderne chairs at an MGM sale in Hollywood, California. Originally from the back lot of the Fred Astaire and Ginger Rogers film *Roberta*, they are now quite at home in the formal dining room and adjoining breakfast room in this Palm Beach residence.

Americans have long emulated the traditional European aesthetic when choosing the manner in which to appoint their homes -- whether the impetus springs from a true reflection of their desires or a cautious need for validation, one cannot be sure. Fortunately, that sense of being bound by historical restraints has lifted, and a newfound freedom and dramatic individualism is now prevalent within many homes. Geoffrey Bradfield captured evidence of this 'freedom' at work in the interior of this contemporary residence in Palm Beach. The designer chose bold color palettes because of the pervasive sunlight that fills the dramatic windows throughout the house. Like a sun worshipper, he employed a vibrant spectrum of hues. There are many exciting ways to give life and glamour to mere walls. Bradfield used a disarmingly simple ragging treatment in a shade of cantaloupe. The eye-catching application makes the space both luxurious and welcoming.

The house is comprised of a series of pavilions connected by long corridors, the largest of which is the living room with eighteen-foot ceilings surrounded by walls of glass. The dazzling 20th century canvas by artist Joan Mitchell over the piano was an added inspiration for the cantaloupe colored walls and matching furnishings against white sofas and antique chairs. The four gilded 18th century bergeres were a rare find and added formal grandeur to the otherwise contemporary arrangement. The bronze sculpture is by artist Lynn Chadwick.

KIRKLAND HOUSE

At left, Bradfield used a Pompeian fresco as a canvas for the Raymond Subes steel and marble console on the elevator landing. The designer accented the doorways with a brushed steel nautical rope. The 19th century kilim formerly belonged to the legendary ballet dancer Rudolf Nureyev.

One enters a seamless world of endless summer in a 3,000 square foot Palm Beach retreat. Geoffrey Bradfield has transformed this apartment overlooking Worth Avenue and the beaches into a floating contemporary palace. Components of the grand design can be seen up close in the entrance hall, with an aqua, ultrasuede fabric providing a stunning backdrop for a Ming Dynasty chair. Against these gem-colored walls, Bradfield has paired Alexander Calder's 'Giraffe' watercolor with Pablo Picasso's pencil drawing of his wife, Jackie.

Mirrors are cleverly employed to disguise the fact that this room, executed in Egyptian granite, is only five feet by seven feet. A pair of Murano wall sconces of terrapins and underwater urchins from the 1950's ornament the walls of this fantastical, seemingly sub-oceanic powder room. Below, the master bedroom is immersed in the same aquatic atmosphere, with a quilted seashell silk as a bed cover and matching draperies. Reflected in the mirror is a watercolor beach scene by Milton Avery.

On the preceding pages: After leaving the entrance hall, one enters the apartment's forty-foot rectangular living room and is greeted with a spectacular view of the sea. Bradfield felt the dimensions of the vast room called for an architectural interruption to lend visual interest. "It was such a long yawn of a room, I had to break it up," the designer recalls. "I designed two pairs of columns and placed them one third from the end of the room. The break allows the eyes to rest." The columns help shape and structure the room, aided by the ceiling-high mouldings and cove lighting. Working with a palette that echoed the aqua shades of the sea, Bradfield masterfully orchestrated a collection of furnishings by Raymond Subes and Gilbert Poillerat. Art and sculpture by Keith Haring, Frank Stella, Fernando Botero and Niki de Saint Phalle complete the scene. On the floor, unifying the palette, is an exceptional Anglo-Indian palace rug.

AN ANSONIA BEDROOM FOR YOUNG GENTLEMEN

A 17th century heroic suit of armor submits to lesser service as a tie rack in the twins' bedroom. Bradfield repeated the heraldic reference throughout the room, from the crenelated battlements atop the bookcase dividing the two beds, on through the ceiling bands of hand-painted coats of arms and the upholstery of the ottoman, which also doubles as a cleverly disguised toy chest.

Standing as a proud landmark on New York's legendary Broadway, the Ansonia Building, designed in 1904 by Paul E.M. Duboy, has been home to legions of great musicians, including the famed masters Stravinsky, Toscanini, Enrico Caruso and, more recently, a pair of seven-year-old twins. With the thought that "a young man's room is his castle," Geoffrey Bradfield devised a playful design of colorful pageantry, utilizing heraldry at every opportunity: "Even the lantern is designed as though it were a royal crown."

A GAME ROOM FOR THE KIPS BAY SHOWHOUSE

Geoffrey Bradfield confesses that his design conceit in this room was the continued architectural reference to the broken pediment which can be found to the left at the top of the mirror and the back of the sofa, and on the following pages in the Roman shade and the upper portion of the hydraulic television cabinet.

The annual Kips Bay Showhouse in New York is a definitive rite of passage for emerging designers and is a wonderful opportunity for them to 'push the envelope.' Few designers of national recognition are not alumni of this professional showcase. Geoffrey Bradfield's game room, illustrated here, weaves together an amalgam of architectural references with intensely colorful beaded Cameroon furniture and *objets d'art*. The lively striped 19th century kilim creates an exciting synergy with the beige and ivory striped walls and upholstery. A portfolio of watercolors by Greg Constantine completes the picture.

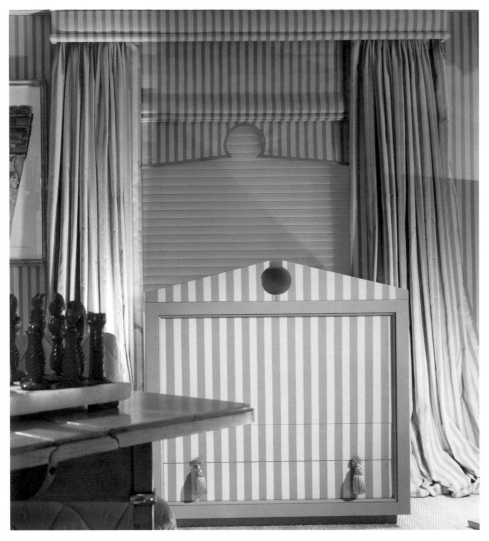

Bradfield designed the television to remain encased within the pediment. In the upper image to the left, the pediment is shown in the closed position, and in the photograph at right it is shown after having been hydraulically opened. Note how the designer's use of striped fabric appears in the upholstered walls, ceiling, sofa and chair, and in the draperies and Roman shades.

A Designer's Flat at the Sherry-Netherland

While completing a project in Manhattan for movie producer Cy Howard and his wife Barbara, the daughter of Jack Warner, Geoffrey Bradfield was introduced to Cecil Beaton, who designed the Oscar-winning sets for *My Fair Lady*, among other Warner Brothers films. At that time Mr. Beaton was leasing a tiny section of the Warner duplex in the Sherry-Netherland Hotel. Bradfield was completely seduced by the building's charm and pledged, "One day I will live in the Sherry-Netherland." And so he did.

Bradfield's apartment on the 22nd floor had not been touched since 1948, so the designer's initial step was to approach the New York Landmarks Commission for permission to install glass doors opening up to the terrace. He then began introducing symmetry to the existing architecture, installing a mirror to lend ballast to the entry opening, and adding six classical pilasters. A virtuoso at blending the best of the past and present, Bradfield has created a veritable showcase of 20th century design, expertly orchestrating periods and styles, beginning with the Art Nouveau movement and progressing right through to the millennium.

An atmosphere of celebration and expectancy pervades Bradfield's apartment. The designer employed a 1930's theme of cool gray and white shades in tandem with subtle, subdued lighting to create a feeling of sleek sophistication.

Bradfield describes the living room, on the following pages, as being "reminiscent of a first class state-room on a great ocean liner." The fashion world's revival of gray flannels influenced the designer to work with a gray and white scheme. The understated yet luxuriantly rich walls, covered with a textured gray raw silk, are the perfect backdrop to works of art by Louise Bourgeois, Lynn Chadwick, Louise Nevelson, Tamara de Lempicka, Jim Dine, Ernest Trova, Hess and Robert Graham; the muted walls also help offset the dramatic lines of the furniture. The bedroom suite is comprised of two bathrooms and a small study with dramatic cityscape views. Says Bradfield, "Interior design should always deal with interpreting the times in which we live. A space ought to be a visual summing up, even if the design concept is an invention of the self: a past, a future, a life, a style."

SELECTED RENDERINGS . . .

The luxurious residence of an industrialist in Mexico City, overlooking Chapultepec Park. A double-volume art-filled entrance hall with a sweeping glass, steel and concrete staircase. Louise Nevelson's monumental wall construction dominates the scene.

The octagonal entrance to the Gungör showroom in Istanbul, Turkey. Bradfield created an open-plan environmental space covering 10,000 square feet on one level. To dramatic effect, he used contrasting brushed steel and scarlet lacquer with high-tech lighting.

One of two reception rooms in a 7,000 square-foot bi-lateral conversion in Eaton Square, London. A double-volume, embassy-scale entrance hall on the first level, is one of five major areas Bradfield integrated, allowing a cohesive flow for optimum entertaining in this sumptuous environment.

The library of a 30,000 square-foot home in Ohio. Bradfield took his inspiration for the paneling from Jansen's masterpiece, his famed library in Madrid. The floors are 18th century parquet de Versailles. Handsome Russian furniture and art by Dubuffet, Leger and van Dongen add color and texture to the masculine setting.

SELECTED PRODUCTS . . .
. . . FROM THE GEOFFREY BRADFIELD COLLECTION

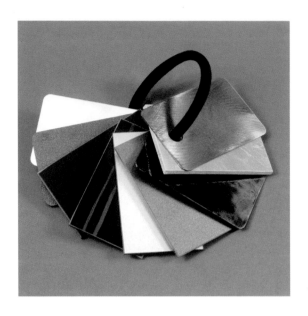

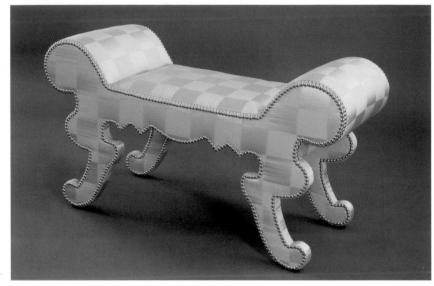

A spectrum of finishes for his thirty-six piece collection of furnishings -- available in Lucite, brushed steel and exotic woods. At right, transcending centuries, a stylish baroque bench re-evaluated in a contemporary checkered silk, edged in steel nailheads.

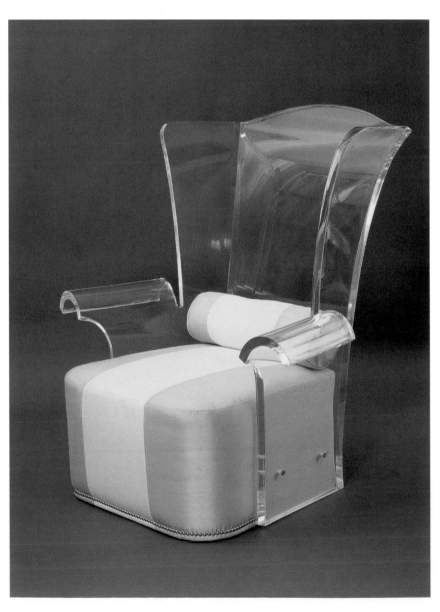

A signature piece in his collection, Bradfield's definitive re-interpretation of a classic: the wingback chair aglow in transparent Lucite. Inspired by the metal work of Art Moderne master Gilbert Poillerat, Geoffrey Bradfield has designed his collection of textiles and carpets to reflect the rhythms of the 1940's with his inimitable touch.

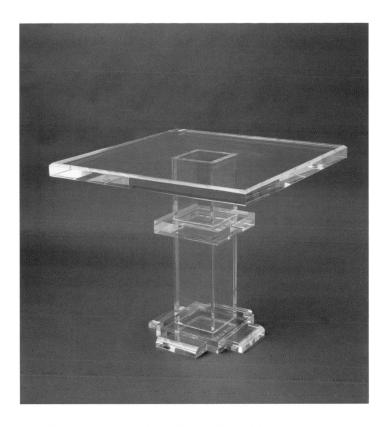

Bradfield has drawn from the 1940's with a unique Contemporary twist . . . influenced by Grosfield House, this chair takes on new vigor in ivory lacquer and white gold. The chair is also available in Lucite and brushed steel.

Capitalizing on his passion for highly reflective surfaces, Bradfield has applied Eastern overtones to a sophisticated collection of tables in Lucite and brushed steel.

THE GEOFFREY BRADFIELD DESIGN TEAM . . .

Bradfield's associate, Company Vice President Douglas Wittels with key players -- eight designers together with support staff keep the selective number of private commissions, commercial designs and follow-up details running on time and on track. To Bradfield and his entire creative team, the future appears limitless in possibilites for new designs, new applications, and bold new creativity.

CREATIVE CREDITS . . .

"There is no civilization worthy of that name without art."

- A. Kisselgoff

fin.